FAST BRAIN, CONFIDENT SPEECH

9

Secrets to Unlocking Success in On-the-Spot Conversations

PHILLIP J. RICHMOND

Please consider writing a review!

Dedication

To all the curious minds who want to master the art of on-the-spot conversations, this book is for you. May you find the secrets to unlocking your fast brain and confident speech, and may you use them to achieve your personal and professional goals.

Also By Phillip J. Richmond

CONTENTS

The key to mastering on-the-spot conversations is not to have all the answers, but to ask the right questions. Questions spark curiosity, curiosity fuels creativity, and creativity leads to innovation

INTRODUCTION

I was always fascinated by people who could think fast and talk smart. People who could come up with witty responses, clever arguments, and captivating stories on the spot. People who could handle any situation with confidence, charisma, and charm. People who could influence, persuade, and inspire others with their words. I wanted to be like them. But I was not.

I was shy, quiet, and insecure. I struggled to express myself, to articulate my thoughts, to make my voice heard. I often felt awkward, nervous, or embarrassed when I had to speak in front of others. I missed many opportunities, both personal and professional, because of my lack of communication skills. I knew I had to change. I knew I had to improve. I knew I had to learn. And so I did.

I read books, watched videos, listened to podcasts, attended workshops, and joined clubs. I studied the techniques, strategies, and secrets of the best speakers, thinkers, and communicators in the world. I practiced, experimented, and applied what I learned in real-life situations. I challenged myself, pushed myself, and surprised myself. And it worked.

I became more confident, more fluent, more eloquent. I became more creative, more adaptable, more persuasive. I became more successful, more fulfilled, more happy. And you can too.

In this book, I will share with you the 9 secrets that I discovered and mastered to unlock my potential and achieve my goals in on-the-spot conversations. These secrets are not only based on my personal experience, but also on scientific research, expert advice, and proven results. These secrets are not only applicable to specific scenarios, but also to any situation where you have to think fast and talk smart. These secrets are not only useful, but also fun, easy, and enjoyable to learn and practice.

These secrets are:

- **Secret 1: Prepare in advance:** Learn how to anticipate, research, and rehearse the topics, questions, and scenarios that you are likely to encounter in your conversations.

- **Secret 2: Relax and breathe:** Learn how to calm your nerves, control your emotions, and manage your stress before and during your conversations.

- **Secret 3: Listen actively and attentively:** Learn how to pay attention, show interest, and understand the needs, wants, and feelings of your conversation partners.

- **Secret 4: Think critically and creatively:** Learn how to analyze, evaluate, and synthesize the information, ideas, and arguments that you hear and generate in your conversations.

- **Secret 5: Adapt and adjust:** Learn how to be flexible, versatile, and responsive to the changing dynamics, expectations, and challenges of your conversations.

- **Secret 6: Be concise and clear:** Learn how to express yourself in a simple, direct, and effective way, without rambling, repeating, or confusing your listeners.

- **Secret 7: Be positive and polite:** Learn how to be friendly, respectful, and courteous in your conversations, without being rude, offensive, or aggressive.

- **Secret 8: Be assertive and persuasive:** Learn how to stand up for yourself, defend your opinions, and convince others to agree with you or take action in your conversations, without being passive, submissive, or manipulative.

- **Secret 9: Be memorable and memorable:** Learn how to make a lasting impression, leave a positive mark, and create a strong connection with your conversation partners, without being boring, forgettable, or irrelevant.

By the end of this book, you will have the knowledge, skills, and confidence to master any on-the-spot conversation that you face in your life. You will be able to think fast and talk smart in various situations, such as:

- **Job interviews:** You will be able to impress your potential employers, showcase your strengths, and land your dream job.

- **Presentations:** You will be able to captivate your audience, deliver your message, and achieve your purpose.

- **Negotiations:** You will be able to bargain, compromise, and reach a win-win outcome.

- **Debates:** You will be able to argue, refute, and win over your opponents.

- **Dates:** You will be able to flirt, charm, and attract your romantic interest.

- **Casual conversations:** You will be able to socialize, network, and make new friends. And much more.

This book is not only for people who want to improve their communication skills, but also for people who want to improve their lives. Because communication is not only a skill, but also a tool. A tool that can help you achieve your goals, fulfill your dreams, and make a difference in the world.

Are you ready to unleash your fast brain and confident speech?

Are you ready to unlock your success in on-the-spot conversations?

Are you ready to start your journey with me? Let's go.

Secret 1: Prepare in advance

You are about to enter a meeting room where you will have to pitch your idea to a group of potential investors. You feel nervous and unsure of yourself. You wonder if you have done enough research, if you know your audience well, and if you can handle any objections or questions they might have. You wish you had more time to prepare, but it is too late now. You have to face the challenge and hope for the best.

But what if you could have done more to prepare in advance? What if you could have used some simple strategies to boost your confidence and improve your performance in any on-the-spot conversation? What if you could have learned the secrets of fast brain, confident speech?

In this chapter, you will discover the first secret to unlocking success in on-the-spot conversations:

prepare in advance. You will learn how to research your topic, audience, and purpose before any conversation, how to anticipate possible questions, challenges, and opportunities, and how to rehearse and practice your responses. By following these steps, you will be able to reduce your anxiety, increase your credibility, and impress your listeners with your knowledge and skills.

Research your topic, audience, and purpose

The first step to prepare in advance is to research your topic, audience, and purpose. This will help you to understand what you are talking about, who you are talking to, and why you are talking.

Research your topic

Researching your topic means gathering relevant and reliable information about the subject matter of your conversation. You can use various sources, such as books, articles, websites, podcasts, videos, or experts, to learn more about your topic. You can also use your own experience, knowledge, or opinions, as long as they are supported by evidence.

The amount and depth of research you need to do depends on the complexity and importance of your topic, as well as the time and resources you have available. However, you should always aim to cover the following aspects:

- The main points or arguments you want to make or support

- The facts, statistics, examples, or stories you want to use to illustrate or back up your points or arguments

- The counterarguments or objections you might encounter or need to address

- The questions or gaps you might have or need to fill

By researching your topic, you will be able to:

- Demonstrate your expertise and credibility

- Provide accurate and relevant information

- Address different perspectives and viewpoints

- Avoid or correct any mistakes or misunderstandings

Research your audience

Researching your audience means finding out as much as you can about the people you are talking to. You can use various methods, such as surveys, interviews, observations, or online profiles, to learn more about your audience. You can also use your own intuition, assumptions, or stereotypes, as long as they are based on evidence and not biased or prejudiced.

The amount and depth of research you need to do depends on the size and diversity of your audience, as well as the context and purpose of your conversation. However, you should always aim to cover the following aspects:

- The demographics of your audience, such as age, gender, education, occupation, culture, or background
- The psychographics of your audience, such as interests, values, beliefs, attitudes, or motivations
- The needs, expectations, or goals of your audience, such as what they want to learn, achieve, or gain from your conversation
- The prior knowledge, experience, or opinions of your audience, such as what they already know, have done, or think about your topic

By researching your audience, you will be able to:

- Adapt your language and style to suit your audience
- Appeal to your audience's emotions and logic
- Address your audience's concerns and objections

- Engage your audience's attention and interest

Research your purpose

Researching your purpose means clarifying the reason or goal of your conversation. You can use various tools, such as SMART goals, SWOT analysis, or logic models, to define and refine your purpose. You can also use your own vision, mission, or values, as long as they are aligned with your topic and audience.

The amount and depth of research you need to do depends on the scope and impact of your purpose, as well as the opportunities and challenges you face. However, you should always aim to cover the following aspects:

- The specific, measurable, achievable, relevant, and time-bound (SMART) objectives you want to accomplish or contribute to

- The strengths, weaknesses, opportunities, and threats (SWOT) you have or face in relation to your purpose

- The inputs, outputs, outcomes, and impacts (logic model) you need or expect to produce or generate from your conversation

By researching your purpose, you will be able to:

- Focus your message and content on your purpose

- Highlight your value and benefits to your audience

- Overcome or mitigate any risks or challenges

- Evaluate your performance and results

Anticipate possible questions, challenges, and opportunities

The second step to prepare in advance is to anticipate possible questions, challenges, and opportunities. This will help you to be ready for any situation or scenario that might arise during your conversation. You can use various techniques, such as brainstorming, mind mapping, or scenario planning, to generate and organize your ideas. You can also use your own imagination, creativity, or curiosity, as long as they are realistic and relevant.

The amount and depth of anticipation you need to do depends on the uncertainty and variability of your conversation, as well as the stakes and consequences you face. However, you should always aim to cover the following aspects:

- The questions you might be asked or need to ask, such as clarifying, probing, challenging, or follow-up questions
- The challenges you might encounter or need to overcome, such as objections, disagreements, misunderstandings, or conflicts

- The opportunities you might find or need to seize, such as openings, connections, collaborations, or innovations

By anticipating possible questions, challenges, and opportunities, you will be able to:

- Prepare your answers and responses in advance
- Handle any difficulties or problems with confidence
- Exploit any advantages or possibilities with enthusiasm
- Adapt to any changes or surprises with flexibility

Rehearse and practice your responses

The third step to prepare in advance is to rehearse and practice your responses. This will help you to polish your delivery and improve your skills in any on-the-spot conversation. You can use various methods, such as recording, feedback, or coaching, to test and refine your responses. You can also use your own self-evaluation, reflection, or learning, as long as they are honest and constructive.

The amount and depth of rehearsal and practice you need to do depends on the difficulty and importance of your conversation, as well as the feedback and support you have available. However, you should always aim to cover the following aspects:

- The verbal and non-verbal aspects of your delivery, such as your voice, tone, pace, volume, pitch, or gestures, eye contact, posture, or facial expressions

- The content and structure of your responses, such as your main points, arguments, evidence, or examples, or your introduction, body, or conclusion

- The timing and sequencing of your responses, such as how long, how often, or how soon you speak, or how you transition, link, or summarize your responses

- The interaction and engagement of your responses, such as how you listen, acknowledge, or respond to your audience, or how you ask, answer, or handle questions, challenges, or opportunities

By rehearsing and practicing your responses, you will be able to:

- Enhance your presentation and communication skills
- Fine-tune your message and content for your purpose
- Optimize your timing and sequencing for your audience
- Increase your interaction and engagement with your listeners

In summary, you have learned the first secret to unlocking success in on-the-spot conversations: prepare in advance. You have discovered how to research your topic, audience, and purpose before any conversation, how to anticipate possible questions, challenges, and opportunities, and how to rehearse and practice your responses. By applying these steps, you will be able to master the art of fast brain, confident speech.

Secret 2: Relax and breathe

You have prepared well for your conversation, and you know what you want to say and how to say it. But as soon as you start speaking, you feel your heart racing, your palms sweating, and your voice trembling. You are nervous and anxious, and you worry that you will mess up or forget something. You feel like you are losing control, and you wish you could just disappear.

Does this sound familiar? If so, you are not alone. Many people experience nervousness and anxiety when they have to speak in front of others, especially in on-the-spot situations. Nervousness and anxiety are natural and normal reactions to stress and uncertainty, and they can actually help you to perform better by boosting your energy and alertness. However, if they become too intense or overwhelming, they can also hinder your performance by affecting your focus, memory, and confidence.

That is why the second secret to unlocking success in on-the-spot conversations is to relax and breathe. By relaxing and breathing, you will be able to:

- Overcome nervousness and anxiety that can hinder your performance
- Use breathing techniques and body language to calm yourself and project confidence
- Cope with unexpected situations and handle mistakes gracefully

Let's look at each of these steps in more detail.

Overcome nervousness and anxiety that can hinder your performance

The first step to relaxing and breathing is to overcome nervousness and anxiety that can hinder your performance. This will help you to:

- Recognize and accept your feelings and thoughts.

- Challenge and reframe your negative beliefs and assumptions.

- Focus on the positive aspects and outcomes of the situation.

For example, before speaking to the investors, you might feel nervous and anxious, and you might think:

- I am not good enough or qualified enough to do this.

- The investors will not like me or my proposal.

- I will make a fool of myself or ruin everything.

These are examples of negative beliefs and assumptions that can make you feel more stressed and insecure. To overcome them, you should:

- Recognize and accept your feelings and thoughts: Acknowledge that you are feeling nervous and anxious, and that it is normal and natural. Don't try to suppress or deny your emotions, as this can make them worse. Instead, accept them as part of the process, and remind yourself that they will pass.

- Challenge and reframe your negative beliefs and assumptions: Question the validity and accuracy of your negative beliefs and assumptions, and look for evidence that contradicts or supports them. For instance, ask yourself: Is it true that I am not good enough or qualified enough? What are my strengths and achievements? Is it true that the investors will not like me or my proposal? What are the benefits and value of my proposal? Is it true that I will make a fool of myself or ruin everything? What are the chances and consequences of that happening?

- Focus on the positive aspects and outcomes of the situation: Instead of dwelling on the worst-case scenarios or the potential problems, focus on the best-case scenarios or the potential opportunities. For example, think about: How will I feel when I succeed in this conversation? What will I learn from this experience? How will this help me to grow and improve?

By overcoming nervousness and anxiety, you will be able to reduce your stress and increase your confidence, and prepare yourself for the conversation.

Use breathing techniques and body language to calm yourself and project confidence

The second step to relaxing and breathing is to use breathing techniques and body language to calm yourself and project confidence. This will help you to:

- Control your physical and mental state and avoid panic
- Communicate your message and personality effectively and authentically

- Connect with your listeners and build rapport and trust

For example, before and during speaking to the investors, you should use:

- **Breathing techniques:** Breathing is one of the most powerful and simple ways to calm yourself and regulate your emotions. By breathing deeply and slowly, you can lower your heart rate, blood pressure, and muscle tension, and increase your oxygen intake, brain activity, and mood. To practice breathing techniques, you can: Inhale through your nose for four seconds, hold your breath for four seconds, exhale through your mouth for four seconds, and repeat for a few minutes. You can also use apps or devices that guide you through different breathing exercises and patterns.

- **Body language:** Body language is one of the most important and influential aspects of communication, as it conveys your attitude, emotions, and intentions, and affects how others perceive and respond to you. By using positive and confident body language, you can enhance your message and personality, and make a good impression. To use positive and confident body language, you should: Smile and make eye contact with your listeners, keep your posture straight and open, use gestures and movements that match and emphasize your words, avoid fidgeting or touching your face or hair, and mirror or match the body language of your listeners.

By using breathing techniques and body language, you will be able to calm yourself and project confidence, and communicate effectively and authentically.

Cope with unexpected situations and handle mistakes gracefully

The third and final step to relaxing and breathing is to cope with unexpected situations and handle mistakes gracefully. This will help you to:

- Adapt to changing circumstances and improvise solutions

- Recover from errors and setbacks and maintain your credibility

- Learn from feedback and criticism and improve your performance

For example, during speaking to the investors, you might encounter:

- **Unexpected situations:** These are situations that you did not anticipate or prepare for, such as technical issues, interruptions, distractions, or changes in the agenda or the audience. These situations can disrupt your flow and throw you off balance, and make you feel frustrated or embarrassed. To cope with them, you should: Stay calm and composed, and don't let them affect your mood or confidence. Acknowledge and address the situation, and apologize or explain if necessary. Adjust your plan and strategy, and adapt to the new circumstances. For instance, if your presentation slides are not working, you can use a flip chart or a handout instead, or just speak without any visual aids.

- **Mistakes:** These are errors or mistakes that you make during the conversation, such as forgetting or mispronouncing a word, giving incorrect or incomplete information, or contradicting yourself or your partner. These mistakes can damage your message and credibility, and make you feel ashamed or guilty. To handle them, you should: Don't panic or dwell on them, and don't let them affect your focus or confidence. Admit and correct your mistakes, and apologize or clarify if necessary. Move on and continue with your message, and don't repeat or emphasize your mistakes. For example, if you say the wrong name or number, you can say: "Sorry, I meant to say John, not James" or "Sorry, I meant to say 50, not 15".

By coping with unexpected situations and handling mistakes gracefully, you will be able to adapt and recover, and maintain your credibility and performance.

Relaxing and breathing is the second secret to unlocking success in on-the-spot conversations. By relaxing and breathing, you will be able to overcome nervousness and anxiety, use breathing techniques and body language, and cope with unexpected situations and handle mistakes gracefully. This will help you to perform better and enjoy the conversation.

Remember: the more you relax and breathe, the better you speak. So, start relaxing and breathing today, and get ready to succeed in any conversation.

The secret to unlocking success in on-the-spot conversations is not to memorize scripts, but to improvise stories. Stories connect, inspire, and persuade people more than facts and figures.

Secret 3: Listen actively and attentively

You have relaxed and breathed, and you are ready to speak. But before you open your mouth, you need to do something else: you need to listen. Listening is not just a passive or polite act, but an active and essential skill for any successful conversation. Listening is the key to understanding your conversation partner, and to being understood by them.

The third secret to unlocking success in on-the-spot conversations is to listen actively and attentively. By listening actively and attentively, you will be able to:

- Show interest and respect to your conversation partner.
- Use listening skills to understand their needs, wants, and emotions.

- Use feedback and questions to clarify and confirm your understanding.

Let's look at each of these steps in more detail.

Show interest and respect to your conversation partner

The first step to listening actively and attentively is to show interest and respect to your conversation partner. This will help you to:

- Establish rapport and trust with your conversation partner

- Encourage your conversation partner to open up and share more information

- Avoid interrupting or judging your conversation partner

For example, when speaking to the investors, you should show interest and respect by:

- **Being attentive and focused:** Give your full attention and focus to your conversation partner, and avoid any distractions or interruptions. Turn off or silence your phone, close your laptop, and put away any other devices or materials that might distract you. Make eye contact with your conversation partner, and nod or smile to show that you are listening.

- **Being respectful and courteous:** Treat your conversation partner with respect and courtesy, and acknowledge their value and expertise. Use their name and title, and address them appropriately. Thank them for their time and attention, and apologize for any inconvenience or delay. Don't argue or criticize your conversation partner, or make any assumptions or stereotypes about them.

- **Being interested and curious:** Show genuine interest and curiosity in your conversation partner, and their thoughts and opinions. Ask open-ended questions that invite them to elaborate and explain. Express appreciation and admiration for their achievements and contributions. Compliment them on their strengths and skills.

By showing interest and respect to your conversation partner, you will be able to create a positive and comfortable atmosphere, and make your conversation partner feel valued and respected.

Use listening skills to understand their needs, wants, and emotions

The second step to listening actively and attentively is to use listening skills to understand their needs, wants, and emotions. This will help you to:

- Identify and empathize with your conversation partner's perspective and situation

- Discover and address your conversation partner's problems and goals

- Adapt and tailor your message and strategy to suit your conversation partner's preferences and expectations

For example, when speaking to the investors, you should use listening skills to understand:

- **Their perspective and situation:** What is their background and experience? What is their role and responsibility? What is their current situation and challenge?

- **Their problems and goals:** What are their pain points and frustrations? What are their needs and wants? What are their aspirations and ambitions?

- **Their preferences and expectations:** What are their values and beliefs? What are their likes and dislikes? What are their criteria and standards?

By using listening skills to understand their needs, wants, and emotions, you will be able to relate and connect with your conversation partner, and offer them relevant and valuable solutions.

Use feedback and questions to clarify and confirm your understanding

The third and final step to listening actively and attentively is to use feedback and questions to clarify and confirm your understanding. This will help you to:

- Avoid misunderstandings and miscommunications that can lead to confusion or conflict.

- Confirm and validate your conversation partner's feelings and thoughts

- Demonstrate your comprehension and interest in your conversation partner's message

For example, when speaking to the investors, you should use feedback and questions to:

- **Avoid misunderstandings and miscommunications**: Repeat or rephrase what your conversation partner said, and ask them to confirm or correct it. For instance, you can say: "So, if I understood correctly, you are looking for a solution that can reduce your costs and increase your efficiency. Is that right?" or "Let me make sure I got this right. You are interested in our proposal, but you have some concerns about the risks and returns. Did I miss anything?"

- **Confirm and validate your conversation partner's feelings and thoughts:** Acknowledge and empathize with your conversation partner's emotions and opinions, and express your agreement or support. For example, you can say: "I can see why you are frustrated with your current situation. It must be very stressful and challenging." or "I agree with your point of view. You have a very valid and reasonable argument."

- **Demonstrate your comprehension and interest in your conversation partner's message:** Ask follow-up questions that show that you have listened and understood your conversation partner's message, and that you want to learn more. For instance, you can say: "That's very interesting. Can you tell me more about how you achieved that result?" or "That's very impressive. How did you overcome that obstacle?"

By using feedback and questions to clarify and confirm your understanding, you will be able to ensure that you and your conversation partner are on the same page, and that you have listened actively and attentively.

Listening actively and attentively is the third secret to unlocking success in on-the-spot conversations. By listening actively and attentively, you will be able to show interest and respect to your conversation partner, use listening skills to understand their needs, wants, and emotions, and use feedback and questions to clarify and confirm your understanding. This will help you to communicate effectively and persuasively, and to achieve your goals.

Remember: the more you listen, the better you speak. So, start listening today, and get ready to succeed in any conversation.

The best way to overcome the fear of on-the-spot conversations is not to avoid them, but to embrace them. Every conversation is an opportunity to learn, grow, and make an impact.

Secret 4: Think critically and creatively

Imagine you are in a meeting with your boss and a potential client. The client has just presented their proposal, and you have some doubts about its feasibility and effectiveness. How do you express your concerns without offending the client or undermining your boss?

This is a common scenario that requires you to think critically and creatively. Critical thinking is the ability to use logic and reasoning to analyze and evaluate information. Creative thinking is the ability to use imagination and humor to generate and express original ideas. Both skills are essential for successful on-the-spot conversations, as they help you to:

- Understand the situation and the perspectives of others

- Identify the strengths and weaknesses of arguments and evidence

- Generate alternative solutions and perspectives

- Communicate your thoughts clearly and persuasively

In this chapter, we will explore some strategies and techniques to enhance your critical and creative thinking skills. We will also show you how to use metaphors and stories to illustrate and persuade your points. By applying these skills, you will be able to impress your boss, win over the client, and boost your confidence in any conversation.

How to use logic and reasoning to analyze and evaluate information

Logic and reasoning are the foundations of critical thinking. They help you to examine the validity and soundness of arguments and evidence, and to avoid logical fallacies and cognitive biases. Here are some steps to apply logic and reasoning in your conversations:

- **Clarify the issue and the goal:** Before you engage in a conversation, make sure you understand what the issue is and what you want to achieve. For example, in the meeting scenario, the issue is whether the client's proposal is suitable for your company, and the goal is to reach a mutually beneficial agreement.

- **Ask questions and gather information:** To evaluate the client's proposal, you need to ask relevant questions and gather sufficient information. For example, you can ask about the client's background, experience, methodology, data sources, assumptions, costs, benefits, risks, and alternatives. You can also do some research on your own to verify the information and fill in the gaps.

- **Identify and challenge assumptions:** Assumptions are beliefs or statements that are taken for granted without evidence. They can be explicit or implicit, and they can affect the quality and validity of arguments and evidence. For example, the client may assume that their proposal is the best option for your company, or that their data is accurate and reliable. You need to identify and challenge these assumptions by asking for evidence or providing counterexamples.

- **Evaluate arguments and evidence:** Arguments are claims that are supported by evidence. Evidence is any information that can be used to prove or disprove a claim. You need to evaluate the arguments and evidence presented by the client, as well as your own, by applying the following criteria:

i. **Relevance:** The evidence should be directly related to the claim and the issue. For example, if the client claims that their proposal will increase your sales, the evidence should show how their proposal will affect your sales, not your brand awareness or customer satisfaction.

ii. **Accuracy:** The evidence should be factual, precise, and consistent. For example, if the client uses statistics or figures, they should be correct, exact, and in agreement with other sources.

iii. **Sufficiency:** The evidence should be enough to support the claim and the issue. For example, if the client uses a case study or a testimonial, they should provide more than one example or source to demonstrate the generalizability and reliability of their results.

iv. **Authority:** The evidence should come from credible and trustworthy sources. For example, if the client uses an expert opinion or a research report, they should provide the credentials and qualifications of the author or the organization, and the date and location of the publication.

v. **Bias:** The evidence should be objective and fair, and not influenced by personal or ulterior motives. For example, if the client uses a survey or a poll, they should disclose the sample size, the sampling method, the questions asked, and the margin of error.

- **Draw conclusions and make recommendations:** Based on your analysis and evaluation of the arguments and evidence, you need to draw logical conclusions and make reasonable recommendations. For example, you can conclude that the client's proposal is feasible but not effective, and recommend some modifications or alternatives. You should also acknowledge the limitations and uncertainties of your conclusions and recommendations, and invite feedback and suggestions from the client and how to use imagination and humor to generate and express original ideas, and how to use stories and anecdotes to illustrate and persuade your points. We have also provided some examples and tips to apply these skills in the meeting scenario.

By thinking critically and creatively, you will be able to:

- Enhance your understanding and evaluation of the situation and the perspectives of others.

- Generate and communicate novel and useful ideas that are appropriate for the situation.

- Use metaphors, stories, and humor to make your points more clear, memorable, and persuasive.

- Impress your boss, win over the client, and boost your confidence in any conversation.

Secret 5: Adapt and adjust

Tara was nervous. She had been invited to give a presentation at the annual conference of her industry, and she knew it was a big opportunity to showcase her expertise and network with potential clients. She had spent weeks preparing her slides, rehearsing her speech, and anticipating the questions she might face. She felt confident that she had a clear and compelling message to deliver.

But as she walked into the conference hall, she realized that things were not going as planned. The room was much larger than she expected, and it was filled with hundreds of people, many of whom she did not recognize. The previous speaker had run over time, and the audience looked bored and restless. She glanced at the agenda and saw that she had only 15 minutes to speak, instead of the 30 she had prepared for. She felt a surge of panic. How was she going to adapt and adjust to this situation?

She took a deep breath and reminded herself of the secret she had learned from reading Fast Brain, Confident Speech: 9 Secrets to Unlocking Success in On-the-Spot Conversations. The secret was to tailor her message to suit her audience, context, and goal, and to use verbal and nonverbal cues to gauge the reaction and mood of her conversation partner. She also had to modify her tone, style, and pace to match the situation. She decided to follow these steps:

- **First**, she identified her audience. She scanned the room and noticed that there were people from different backgrounds, sectors, and levels of seniority. She realized that she had to make her message relevant and interesting to a diverse group of listeners, and avoid using too much jargon or technical details that might confuse or alienate them.

- **Second**, she assessed the context. She acknowledged that the room was large and noisy, and that the audience was tired and distracted. She realized that she had to capture their attention and keep them engaged, and avoid being too formal or monotone. She also had to respect the time limit and avoid going overboard with her slides or points.

- **Third**, she clarified her goal. She reminded herself that her purpose was to share her insights and experience on a topic that she was passionate about, and to establish her credibility and authority in her field. She also wanted to connect with the audience and invite them to ask questions or follow up with her later. She realized that she had to be clear and concise, and avoid being too vague or humble.

- **Fourth**, she used verbal cues. She listened to the introduction by the moderator and thanked him for the opportunity. She greeted the audience and introduced herself and her topic. She used a catchy hook to grab their interest and a clear roadmap to guide them through her main points. She used stories, examples, and statistics to illustrate her arguments and support her claims. She used transitions, signposts, and summaries to keep them on track and reinforce her message. She used questions, polls, and quizzes to involve them and check their understanding. She used humor, anecdotes, and quotes to entertain them and make them laugh. She used a strong conclusion to recap her main points and call them to action. She used a memorable slogan to leave a lasting impression and invite them to contact her for more information.

- **Fifth**, she used nonverbal cues. She looked at the audience and made eye contact with different people. She smiled and nodded to show her friendliness and enthusiasm. She used gestures and movements to emphasize her points and express her emotions. She used pauses and variations in her voice to create interest and suspense. She used facial expressions and body language to convey her confidence and sincerity. She used props and visual aids to enhance her presentation and appeal to different learning styles.

By following these steps, Tara was able to adapt and adjust to the situation and deliver a successful presentation. The audience was impressed by her knowledge and skills, and they applauded and cheered her at the end. She received many compliments and questions from the attendees, and she exchanged business cards with several potential clients. She felt proud and happy. She had mastered the secret of fast brain, confident speech.

The most powerful conversations are not the ones where you say everything, but the ones where you listen to everything.

Secret 6: Be concise and clear

Imagine you are in a meeting with your boss and colleagues. You have an important idea that you want to share, but you are not sure how to say it. You start talking, but you find yourself rambling on and on, using words that are vague, technical, or redundant. You notice that your audience is losing interest, checking their phones, or looking confused. You feel frustrated and embarrassed, and you wonder why you can't express yourself clearly and confidently.

This is a common scenario that many people face when they have to speak on the spot. Whether it is a meeting, a presentation, a negotiation, or a casual conversation, you want to communicate your message in a way that is easy to understand, engaging, and persuasive. But how do you do that?

The answer is simple: be concise and clear. Concise means using the fewest words possible to convey your meaning. Clear means using the most appropriate words to convey your meaning. Being concise and clear will help you avoid unnecessary words, jargon, and filler phrases that can confuse and bore your listener. It will also help you use simple and direct language that can convey your meaning effectively. And it will help you structure your speech with an introduction, body, and conclusion that can make your message coherent and memorable.

Here are some tips on how to be concise and clear in your on-the-spot speech:

- **Avoid unnecessary words:** Unnecessary words are those that do not add any value or meaning to your message. They can make your speech longer, weaker, and less focused. For example, instead of saying "I think that we should definitely consider the possibility of implementing this new strategy in the near future", you can say "We should implement this new strategy soon". This way, you can eliminate the words "I think that", "definitely", "consider the possibility of", and "in the near future", which are redundant, vague, or too wordy.

- **Avoid jargon:** Jargon is the specialized or technical language that is used by a specific group or profession. It can be useful when you are communicating with people who share the same background or expertise as you, but it can be confusing and alienating when you are communicating with people who do not. For example, instead of saying "We need to leverage our core competencies and optimize our value proposition to achieve a win-win situation with our stakeholders", you can say "We need to use our strengths and offer our best service to satisfy our customers". This way, you can replace the jargon words "leverage", "core competencies", "optimize", "value proposition", and "stakeholders" with simpler and more concrete words that anyone can understand.

- **Avoid filler phrases:** Filler phrases are those that you use to fill the silence or buy time when you are speaking. They can make your speech sound hesitant, unprepared, or unprofessional. For example, instead of saying "Um, you know, like, I mean, basically, what I'm trying to say is that, you know, we have a problem here", you can say "We have a problem here". This way, you can eliminate the filler phrases "um", "you know", "like", "I mean", "basically", and "what I'm trying to say is that", which do not contribute anything to your message.

- **Use simple and direct language:** Simple and direct language is the language that is easy to understand and straightforward. It can make your speech sound clear, confident, and convincing. For example, instead of saying "The reason why we are experiencing this issue is due to the fact that there is a lack of communication between the different departments", you can say "We have this issue because the departments do not communicate well". This way, you can use simpler and more direct words and sentences that can convey your meaning effectively.

- **Structure your speech with an introduction, body, and conclusion:** A good speech has a clear structure that can help you organize your thoughts and guide your listener. An introduction is where you state your main idea and purpose, and capture your listener's attention. A body is where you support your main idea with facts, examples, or arguments. A conclusion is where you summarize your main points and end with a call to action or a memorable statement. For example, if you want to persuade your boss to adopt a new policy, you can structure your speech as follows:

i.   **Introduction**: "I have a proposal that can improve our productivity and morale. It is about allowing flexible work hours for our team."

ii. **Body**: "Flexible work hours can benefit us in three ways. First, it can reduce stress and increase happiness. Second, it can enhance creativity and innovation. Third, it can boost performance and efficiency."

iii. **Conclusion**: "Flexible work hours are a win-win solution for our team and our company. I urge you to approve this policy and let us work in a way that suits our needs and preferences."

Being concise and clear is not only a skill, but also a habit. The more you practice it, the more natural and effortless it will become. By being concise and clear, you can make your on-the-spot speech fast, brainy, and confident. And you can unlock the secret to success in any communication situation.

On-the-spot conversations are not about being perfect, but about being present. When you are fully engaged with the moment, your fast brain and confident speech will follow.

Secret 7: Be positive and polite

One of the most important secrets to unlocking success in on-the-spot conversations is to be positive and polite. This means using words and expressions that can uplift and inspire your listener, as well as showing respect and courtesy to your conversation partner. On the other hand, you should avoid negative words and behaviors that can offend and alienate your listener. In this chapter, we will explore how to do this effectively and why it matters.

Why be positive and polite?

Being positive and polite can have many benefits for your on-the-spot conversations. Here are some of them:

- It can **build rapport** and trust with your listener. When you use positive and polite language, you show that you care about your listener's feelings and opinions, and that you value their input. This can make your listener more receptive and responsive to your message, and more likely to cooperate with you.

- It can **enhance your image** and reputation. When you use positive and polite language, you demonstrate that you are a professional, respectful, and confident person. This can make your listener respect you more, and see you as an authority and a leader. It can also make you stand out from others who may use negative or rude language, and give you an edge in competitive situations.

- It can **improve your mood** and attitude. When you use positive and polite language, you focus on the positive aspects of the situation, and avoid dwelling on the negative ones. This can make you feel more optimistic, hopeful, and motivated, and less stressed, anxious, and frustrated. It can also make you more resilient and adaptable to challenges and changes.

How to be positive and polite?

Being positive and polite is not just about saying "please" and "thank you". It is also about choosing the right words and expressions, and using the right tone and body language, to convey your message in a positive and polite way. Here are some tips on how to do this:

- Use **positive words and expressions** that can uplift and inspire your listener. For example, you can use words and expressions like "great", "wonderful", "amazing", "excellent", "fantastic", "brilliant", "awesome", "well done", "congratulations", "thank you", "I appreciate", "I admire", "I agree", "I understand", "I support", "I'm happy for you", "I'm proud of you", "I'm impressed by you", "you're doing great", "you're awesome", "you're amazing", etc. These words and expressions can make your listener feel good about themselves, and about the situation. They can also show that you are enthusiastic, supportive, and appreciative of your listener.

- Use **polite words and manners** that can show respect and courtesy to your conversation partner. For example, you can use words and manners like "please", "thank you", "excuse me", "sorry", "pardon me", "may I", "could you", "would you mind", "I'm sorry to bother you", "I don't mean to interrupt you", "I hope you don't mind", "I respect your opinion", "I appreciate your feedback", "I value your input", "thank you for your time", "thank you for your patience", "thank you for your cooperation", etc. These words and manners can show that you are considerate, humble, and respectful of your listener's time, space, and feelings. They can also show that you are polite, courteous, and professional.

- Avoid **negative words and behaviors** that can offend and alienate your listener. For example, you should avoid words and behaviors like "no", "never", "can't", "won't", "don't", "shouldn't", "mustn't", "bad", "terrible", "horrible", "awful", "stupid", "idiot", "loser", "failure", "hate", "dislike", "disagree", "blame", "criticize", "complain", "argue", "yell", "interrupt", "ignore", "roll your eyes", "cross your arms", "frown", "sigh", etc. These words and behaviors can make your listener feel bad about themselves, and about the situation. They can also show that you are negative, hostile, and disrespectful of your listener.

Examples of being positive and polite

Here are some examples of how to use positive and polite language in different on-the-spot conversation scenarios:

- **Scenario 1:** You are giving feedback to a colleague on their presentation.

- *Negative and rude:* "Your presentation was boring and confusing. You didn't explain anything clearly, and you wasted everyone's time. You need to work on your communication skills."

- *Positive and polite:* "Thank you for your presentation. I appreciate your effort and enthusiasm. I have some suggestions on how you can improve your communication skills. Would you mind if I share them with you?"

- **Scenario 2:** You are asking a question to a speaker at a conference.

- *Negative and rude:* "Your talk was nonsense. You didn't provide any evidence or data to support your claims. How can you expect anyone to believe you?"

- *Positive and polite:* "Thank you for your talk. I admire your passion and creativity. I have a question about your claims. Could you please provide some evidence or data to support them?"

- **Scenario 3:** You are negotiating a deal with a client.

- *Negative and rude:* "Your offer is unacceptable. You are asking for too much, and giving too little. You are being unreasonable and greedy. Take it or leave it."

- *Positive and polite:* "I appreciate your offer. You are a valued and respected client. However, I'm afraid we can't accept it as it is. Could we please discuss some possible alternatives?"

The ultimate goal of on-the-spot conversations is not to win arguments, but to build relationships. Relationships are the foundation of trust, collaboration, and success.

Secret 8: Be assertive and persuasive

One of the most important skills for success in on-the-spot conversations is the ability to be assertive and persuasive. Being assertive means expressing your opinions and preferences confidently, without being passive or aggressive. Being persuasive means using words and techniques that can influence and convince your listener, without being manipulative or coercive.

How to be assertive

Being assertive is not the same as being arrogant or rude. It is about respecting yourself and others, and communicating your needs and wants clearly and respectfully. Here are some tips on how to be assertive in on-the-spot conversations:

- Use **I-statements** to express your feelings, thoughts, and opinions. For example, instead of saying "You are wrong", say "I disagree with you". This way, you avoid blaming or attacking the other person, and focus on your own perspective.

- Use **positive language** to convey your message. For example, instead of saying "Don't do that", say "Please do this". This way, you avoid sounding negative or demanding, and show your appreciation and cooperation.

- Use **assertive body language** to support your words. For example, maintain eye contact, use a firm but friendly tone of voice, and adopt a relaxed but confident posture. This way, you avoid looking nervous or submissive, and show your self-confidence and credibility.

- Use **assertive techniques** to handle difficult situations. For example, if someone interrupts you, say "Excuse me, I was not finished". If someone criticizes you, say "Thank you for your feedback, but I disagree". If someone makes an unreasonable request, say "No, I cannot do that". This way, you avoid being silenced or bullied, and stand up for your rights and boundaries.

How to be persuasive

Being persuasive is not the same as being deceptive or pushy. It is about understanding and appealing to your listener, and creating a win-win situation. Here are some tips on how to be persuasive in on-the-spot conversations:

- Use **facts and evidence** to support your arguments. For example, if you want to convince someone to buy your product, show them the benefits and features, and provide testimonials and statistics. This way, you avoid making vague or unsubstantiated claims, and show your knowledge and credibility.

- Use **emotions and stories** to connect with your listener. For example, if you want to persuade someone to donate to your cause, tell them a personal story, and appeal to their values and feelings. This way, you avoid being dry or impersonal, and show your passion and empathy.

- Use **reciprocity and scarcity** to motivate your listener. For example, if you want to influence someone to agree with your proposal, offer them something in return, and emphasize the urgency and uniqueness of your offer. This way, you avoid being selfish or boring, and show your generosity and value.

- Use **social proof and authority** to validate your position. For example, if you want to sway someone to join your team, show them the popularity and reputation of your team, and cite the opinions and endorsements of experts and influencers. This way, you avoid being isolated or ignored, and show your popularity and trustworthiness.

How to avoid being aggressive

Being aggressive is not the same as being assertive or persuasive. It is about disrespecting and dominating others, and communicating your needs and wants in a hostile and threatening way. Here are some tips on how to avoid being aggressive in on-the-spot conversations:

- Avoid using **you-statements** to accuse or blame the other person. For example, instead of saying "You are stupid", say "I don't understand your point". This way, you avoid hurting or insulting the other person, and focus on the issue, not the person.

- Avoid using **negative language** to belittle or criticize the other person. For example, instead of saying "That's a stupid idea", say "I don't agree with that idea". This way, you avoid being rude or sarcastic, and show your respect and professionalism.

- Avoid using **aggressive body language** to intimidate or challenge the other person. For example, avoid staring, shouting, or invading the other person's personal space. This way, you avoid being scary or violent, and show your calmness and civility.

- Avoid using **aggressive techniques** to manipulate or coerce the other person. For example, avoid interrupting, name-calling, or making threats or ultimatums. This way, you avoid being unfair or abusive, and show your honesty and integrity.

Being assertive and persuasive is not easy, but it is possible. By following these tips, you can improve your communication skills and achieve your goals in on-the-spot conversations. Remember, the key is to be confident, respectful, and convincing, without being passive, aggressive, or manipulative.

You are perfect and a

success.

Secret 9: Be memorable and memorable

You've learned how to prepare, start, and deliver a speech on the spot. But how do you make sure that your speech is not forgotten as soon as you finish? How do you leave a lasting impression on your listeners and persuade them to take action or remember your message? The answer is to be memorable and memorable. This means using memorable words and gestures that can capture your listener's attention and emotion, and using memorable words and strategies that can reinforce and summarize your main points. It also means ending your speech with a call to action or a memorable quote that can inspire your listeners and make them think.

Memorable words are words that are vivid, specific, and powerful. They can create a clear image in your listener's mind and appeal to their senses and emotions. For example, instead of saying "The product is good", you can say "The product is sleek, innovative, and user-friendly". Instead of saying "The situation is bad", you can say "The situation is dire, urgent, and alarming".

Memorable gestures are gestures that are expressive, natural, and appropriate. They can complement your words and enhance your message. For example, you can use your hands to show the size, shape, or direction of something. You can use your facial expressions to convey your emotions or attitudes. You can use your body language to show your confidence or enthusiasm.

To use memorable words and gestures effectively, you need to:

- Know your audience and tailor your words and gestures to their interests, needs, and expectations.

- Know your purpose and choose your words and gestures to support your main idea and goal.

- Know your topic and use your words and gestures to demonstrate your knowledge and credibility.

- Practice your words and gestures and make sure they are clear, accurate, and consistent.

Use memorable words and strategies

Memorable words and strategies are words and techniques that can help you reinforce and summarize your main points. They can help your listener remember and understand your message better. For example, you can use:

- **Repetition:** Repeat your main points or keywords throughout your speech to emphasize them and make them stick in your listener's mind. For example, you can say "The three benefits of our product are: speed, quality, and affordability. Let me explain each benefit in detail. First, speed. Our product is faster than any other product in the market. Second, quality. Our product is more reliable and durable than any other product in the market. Third, affordability. Our product is cheaper than any other product in the market. So, to recap, the three benefits of our product are: speed, quality, and affordability."

- Rhyme: Use words that rhyme or sound similar to create a catchy and memorable phrase or slogan. For example, you can say "A stitch in time saves nine" or "Don't be a fool, stay in school".

- **Alliteration:** Use words that start with the same sound or letter to create a rhythmic and memorable sentence or phrase. For example, you can say "She sells seashells by the seashore" or "Peter Piper picked a peck of pickled peppers".

- **Acronym:** Use the first letters of a series of words to create a memorable word or name. For example, you can say "NASA stands for National Aeronautics and Space Administration" or "SMART stands for Specific, Measurable, Achievable, Relevant, and Time-bound".

- **Mnemonic:** Use a word, phrase, or image that can help you remember a list of items or facts. For example, you can say "ROYGBIV is a mnemonic for the colors of the rainbow: red, orange, yellow, green, blue, indigo, and violet" or "My Very Eager Mother Just Served Us Nine Pizzas is a mnemonic for the order of the planets: Mercury, Venus, Earth, Mars, Jupiter, Saturn, Uranus, Neptune, and Pluto".

To use memorable words and strategies effectively, you need to:

- Use them sparingly and strategically. Don't overuse them or they will lose their impact and become annoying.

- Use them appropriately and relevantly. Don't use them just for the sake of using them or they will distract from your message and confuse your listener.

- Use them creatively and originally. Don't use them clichéd or outdated or they will bore your listener and undermine your credibility.

End with a call to action or a memorable quote

The last part of your speech is the most important part. It is the part that your listener will remember the most and act upon. Therefore, you need to end your speech with a strong and memorable conclusion that can motivate your listener and make them think.

One way to do that is to end your speech with a call to action. A call to action is a statement that urges your listener to do something or to change something. It can be a request, a recommendation, a suggestion, or a command. For example, you can say "If you want to improve your health, fitness, and happiness, join our gym today" or "If you care about the environment, reduce your carbon footprint and recycle your waste".

Another way to do that is to end your speech with a memorable quote. A memorable quote is a statement that expresses a profound or inspiring idea or sentiment. It can be a quote from a famous person, a book, a movie, or a song. For example, you can say "As Mahatma Gandhi once said, 'Be the change that you wish to see in the world'" or "As John Lennon sang, 'Imagine all the people living life in peace'".

To end your speech with a call to action or a memorable quote effectively, you need to:

- Choose a call to action or a quote that is relevant to your topic, purpose, and audience.

- Choose a call to action or a quote that is clear, concise, and powerful.
- Choose a call to action or a quote that is appropriate, respectful, and ethical.
- Deliver your call to action or quote with confidence, passion, and conviction.

Being memorable and memorable is the key to unlocking success in on-the-spot conversations. By using memorable words and gestures, memorable words and strategies, and ending your speech with a call to action or a memorable quote, you can make a lasting impression on your listener and persuade them to take action or remember your message. Remember, the more memorable you are, the more successful you will be.

Conclusion: How to apply the 9 secrets in your everyday life

You have learned the 9 secrets to unlocking success in on-the-spot conversations. These secrets are not just theoretical concepts, but practical skills that you can apply in your everyday life. Whether you want to ace a job interview, impress a client, make a new friend, or simply have a meaningful conversation, these secrets will help you achieve your goals.

Let's recap the 9 secrets and how they can help you:

- **Secret 1: Prepare in advance:** This secret helps you to anticipate the possible topics, questions, and scenarios that you might encounter in a conversation. By preparing in advance, you can reduce your anxiety, boost your confidence, and have more ideas to share.

- **Secret 2: Relax and breathe:** This secret helps you to calm your nerves, control your emotions, and focus your attention. By relaxing and breathing, you can avoid panic, stuttering, and blanking out.

- **Secret 3: Listen actively and attentively:** This secret helps you to understand the other person's perspective, needs, and interests. By listening actively and attentively, you can show respect, empathy, and curiosity.

- **Secret 4: Think critically and creatively:** This secret helps you to analyze the information, generate new insights, and solve problems. By thinking critically and creatively, you can demonstrate your intelligence, creativity, and competence.

- **Secret 5: Adapt and adjust:** This secret helps you to respond to the changing dynamics, expectations, and feedback of the conversation.

By adapting and adjusting, you can be flexible, resilient, and resourceful.

- **Secret 6: Be concise and clear:** This secret helps you to communicate your message effectively, efficiently, and elegantly. By being concise and clear, you can avoid confusion, boredom, and misunderstanding.

- **Secret 7: Be positive and polite:** This secret helps you to create a positive impression, build rapport, and avoid conflict. By being positive and polite, you can express your appreciation, compliment, and apologize.

- **Secret 8: Be assertive and persuasive:** This secret helps you to express your opinions, preferences, and requests confidently, respectfully, and convincingly. By being assertive and persuasive, you can influence, negotiate, and persuade.

- **Secret 9: Be memorable and memorable:** This secret helps you to leave a lasting impression, make an impact, and inspire action. By being memorable and memorable, you can use stories, humor, and call to action.

These secrets have helped me and many others to improve our on-the-spot conversations and achieve success in various aspects of our lives. Here are some examples and testimonials of how these secrets have made a difference:

- **Example 1:** I used to be terrified of public speaking, especially when I had to answer questions from the audience. But after learning the 9 secrets, I was able to prepare in advance, relax and breathe, listen actively and attentively, think critically and creatively, adapt and adjust, be concise and clear, be positive and polite, be assertive and persuasive, and be memorable and memorable. As a result, I delivered a successful presentation at a conference and received a lot of positive feedback and applause.

- **Testimonial 1:** "The 9 secrets have changed my life. I used to struggle with on-the-spot conversations, especially in social situations. I would feel nervous, awkward, and boring. But after applying the 9 secrets, I became more confident, comfortable, and interesting. I made new friends, networked with influential people, and even met my soulmate. Thank you for sharing these secrets with me."

- **Example 2:** I used to have a hard time with on-the-spot conversations, especially in professional settings. I would feel unprepared, overwhelmed, and incompetent. But after practicing the 9 secrets, I became more ready, calm, and capable. I aced a job interview, impressed a client, and solved a problem. As a result, I got a promotion, a raise, and a recognition.

- **Testimonial 2:** "The 9 secrets have transformed my career. I used to dread on-the-spot conversations, especially in challenging situations. I would feel anxious, defensive, and unconvincing. But after implementing the 9 secrets, I became more relaxed, respectful, and persuasive. I influenced a decision, negotiated a deal, and persuaded a stakeholder. As a result, I achieved a goal, saved a project, and earned a trust."

These are just some of the many examples and testimonials of how the 9 secrets have helped me and others to unlock success in on-the-spot conversations. But don't just take my word for it. Try it for yourself. Practice and implement these secrets in your own conversations. You will be amazed by the results. You will have a fast brain, a confident speech, and a successful life.

Gain access to all my previous and future

books

www.ingramcontent.com/pod-product-compliance
Lightning Source LLC
Chambersburg PA
CBHW050035260726
48658CB00005B/1622